CW01402593

Keep this pocket-si
you are visiting Wi
in the locality.

Whether you ar
enjoy an evocative journey back in time. Compare
the Winchester of old with what you can see
today—see how the streets of the city and its parks
and open spaces have changed; examine the shops
and buildings and notice how they have been altered
or replaced; look at fine details such as lamp-posts,
shop fascias and trade signs; and see the many
alterations to Winchester and its surrounding villages
that have taken place unnoticed during our lives,
some of which we may have taken for granted.

At the turn of a page you will gain fascinating
insights into Winchester's unique history.

FRANCIS FRITH'S
pocket ALBUM

WINCHESTER

A POCKET ALBUM

Adapted from an original book by
JOHN BAINBRIDGE

THE FRANCIS FRITH COLLECTION ®

First published in the United Kingdom in 2004 by
Frith Book Company Ltd

ISBN 1-85937-918-4
Text and Design copyright © Frith Book Company Ltd
Photographs copyright © The Francis Frith Collection

British Library Cataloguing in Publication Data

Winchester—A Pocket Album
Adapted from an original book by John Bainbridge

Frith Book Company Ltd
Frith's Barn, Teffont,
Salisbury, Wiltshire SP3 5QP
Tel: +44 (0) 1722 716 376
Email: info@francisfrith.co.uk
www.francisfrith.co.uk

Printed and bound in Great Britain by MPG, Bodmin

Front Cover: WINCHESTER, HIGH ST 1928 80886
The colour-tinting is for illustrative purposes only, and is not intended to be historically accurate.

Frontispiece: WINCHESTER, CATHEDRAL c1960 W107076

WESTGATE 1909 / 62175

CONTENTS

FRANCIS FRITH
VICTORIAN PIONEER

Francis Frith, founder of the world-famous photographic archive, was a complex and multi-talented man. A devout Quaker and a highly successful Victorian businessman, he was philosophic by nature and pioneering in outlook. By 1855 he had already established a wholesale grocery business in Liverpool, and sold it for the astonishing sum of £200,000, which is the equivalent today of over £15,000,000. Now in his thirties, and captivated by the new science of photography, Frith set out on a series of pioneering journeys up the Nile and to the Near East.

INTRIGUE AND EXPLORATION

He was the first photographer to venture beyond the sixth cataract of the Nile. Africa was still the mysterious 'Dark Continent', and Stanley and Livingstone's historic meeting was a decade into the future. The conditions for picture taking confound belief. He laboured for hours in his wicker dark-room in the sweltering heat of the desert, while the volatile chemicals fizzed dangerously in their trays. Back in London he exhibited his photographs and was 'rapturously cheered' by members of the Royal Society. His reputation as a photographer was made overnight.

VENTURE OF A LIFE-TIME

By the 1870s the railways had threaded their way across the country, and Bank Holidays and half-day Saturdays had been made obligatory by Act of Parliament. All of a sudden the working man and his family were able to enjoy days out, take holidays, and see a little more of the world.

With typical business acumen, Francis Frith foresaw that these new tourists would enjoy having souvenirs to commemorate their days out. For the next thirty years he travelled the country by train and by pony and trap, producing fine photographs of seaside resorts and beauty spots that were keenly bought by millions of Victorians. These prints were painstakingly pasted into family albums and pored over during the dark nights of winter, rekindling precious memories of summer excursions. Frith's studio was soon supplying retail shops all over the country, and by 1890 F Frith & Co had become the greatest specialist photographic publishing company in the world, with over 2,000 sales outlets, and pioneered the picture postcard.

FRANCIS FRITH'S LEGACY

Francis Frith had died in 1898 at his villa in Cannes, his great project still growing. The archive he created continued in business for another seventy years. By 1970 it contained over a third of a million pictures showing 7,000 British towns and villages.

Frith's legacy to us today is of immense significance and value, for the magnificent archive of evocative photographs he created provides a unique record of change in the cities, towns and villages throughout Britain over a century and more. Frith and his fellow studio photographers revisited locations many times down the years to update their views, compiling for us an enthralling and colourful pageant of British life and character.

We are fortunate that Frith was dedicated to recording the minutiae of everyday life. For it is this sheer wealth of visual data, the painstaking chronicle of changes in dress, transport, street layouts, buildings, housing, engineering and landscape that captivates us so much today, offering us a powerful link with the past and with the lives of our ancestors.

Computers have now made it possible for Frith's many thousands of images to be accessed almost instantly. The archive offers every one of us an opportunity to examine the places where we and our families have lived and worked down the years. Its images, depicting our shared past, are now bringing pleasure and enlightenment to millions around the world a century and more after his death.

FROM ST GILES HILL 1893 / 32650

WINCHESTER
THE CITY OF KINGS AND PRIESTS

Winchester. The capital city of Wessex is a history lesson in every stone of its streets, for this old place began to play an important role in the nation's past from the time the Romans founded their market town of Venta Belgarum on the site of enclosures left there by the conquered Iron Age tribe, the Belgae, on the banks of the River Itchen.

Though no one knows for certain where the bones of Alfred the Great actually rest, this was the heart of his Wessex; the capital of his old age and a refuge of peace and learning after long years of struggle fending off the Danes. Interestingly, the Anglo-Saxon Chronicle lists very few visits by Alfred to Winchester - perhaps his sojourns there were just taken for granted. His son Edward the Elder, if anything, really deserves the connection and some kind of statue, for it was he who founded the important New Minster that was to be his father's burial place.

Generations earlier in the year 643 a Minster church had been established in the town by Alfred's Saxon forbear Cenwalh. Thirty years later Bishop Haeddi arrived in Winchester and made that building his Cathedral. Alfred the Great was originally buried in the Old Minster of Cenwalh's foundation before his bones were transferred to the New Minster. In the century after his death, Winchester became the most important religious centre in northern Europe.

The Norman Conquest saw the removal of the Saxon Bishop Stigand, his Norman replacement Walkelin beginning the construction of the huge Cathedral we see today on a site roughly adjacent to the Old Minster. The nave, supposedly the longest in Europe, stretches away from the visitor entering at the western end "a vista of magnificence which, almost like the first sight of the sea or the Alps, impresses itself upon the memory for one's life".

A walk along the north aisle brings the visitor to the tomb of Jane Austen. To one side is a commemorative window to this fine novelist and a plaque to remind us of her role in English Letters—something her black marble tombstone fails to do. Nor is she the only writer buried within. Izaak Walton, author of 'The Compleat Angler', that wonderful tribute to contemplation and the English countryside, rests not far away in the Chapel of St John the Evangelist.

"Nowhere in England do the stones speak more eloquently of past times than in Winchester, the city of kings and priests", wrote two Victorian residents. And a fair number of both kings and priests lie with the precincts of the Cathedral; bishops such as William of Edington, and William of Wykeham, the founder of Winchester College and instigator of the reconstructed nave in the 14th century. Swithun, whose elevation to sainthood made Winchester a destination for medieval pilgrims was also originally buried here. Only one miracle is ascribed to Swithun during his lifetime—the restoration of a basket of eggs dropped and smashed by a local woman. But the pilgrims came because of the miracles and cures that are supposed to have happened after the burial of the former bishop.

On the presbytery screens are four mortuary chests (two more are reproductions) containing the bones of Swithun, several ancient Saxon kings, a handful of early bishops and those of King Canute and the unfortunate King William Rufus. During restoration work in the reign of Henry VIII, the bones were reinterred within these caskets, because there was no way of knowing who was who. As the old chronicler says: "Not knowing which were kings and which were bishops, because there were no inscriptions over the monuments…Henry placed in leaden sarcophagi kings and bishops, bishops and kings all mixed together".

There are many other delights within the building, from exquisite wall paintings dating back to the Crusades, to the famous Winchester Bible which dates from the 12th century and is perhaps the finest illustrated book in England. Elsewhere, a flight of steps leads down to the crypt. Given the marshy nature of the ground on which the cathedral stands this often floods after the rains of winter. It is now adorned with a modern statue of a human figure, called Sound II, which often stands in the water.

As we can see from the photographs, the tower is modest in size compared to the towers of many other British cathedrals. In 1107 Bishop Walkelin's original tower collapsed on to the tomb of King William Rufus. Unkind clerics claimed that this was a punishment for the King's dissolute life – but then the medieval church habitually slurred the memory of monarchs who had offended it. The modesty of the tower serves a purpose, for it does not distract the eye from the rest of the architecture and adornments, especially the magnificent west front.

The photographs that follow show the exterior of the Cathedral in all its splendour from the year 1886 to 1960. It has changed very little in the forty years since the last picture was taken, except for the opening of a worthy and informative visitor centre. The peace and tranquillity and the deep sense of history remain. A visit to Winchester should begin here, for this is the best place to grasp the importance, the power and the influence on king and priest on the rest of the city.

The historic heart of old Winchester, once the capital of the Saxon kingdom of Wessex, is seen here from the heights of St Giles hill. The great Norman Cathedral dominates the scene as it has dominated Winchester's history.

FROM ST GILES

1886 / 19401

Winchester lies on the western banks of the River Itchen at a crossing important to Iron Age dwellers thousands of years ago. This was Alfred the Great's capital, and a favoured residence of many English kings and queens.

GENERAL VIEW

1893 / 32648

FROM ST GILES HILL

1893 / 32650

After the Roman invasion of AD43, old Iron Age enclosures were adapted to create the important Roman town of Venta Belgarum. Winchester remained an important settlement until the Romans withdrew in about 410. Much of the street pattern we see here is medieval in origin.

Beyond the water meadows of the River Itchen is the Iron Age hillfort of St Catherine's Hill, the site of a maze which perhaps was used by penitent local monks, who would be blindfolded as they attempted to trace its paths. The view from the hill is one of the finest in Hampshire.

FROM ST CATHERINE'S HILL
1899 / 43675

Looking along Broadway with the statue of Alfred the Great clearly visible, this view shows Winchester Cathedral in all its glory. Notice the army barracks on the hill beyond.

FROM ST GILES HILL
1929 / 81610

A walk from the Square brings the visitor across a green and open space to the Norman Cathedral. Tourists come from all over the world to visit this architectural and spiritual gem.

THE CATHEDRAL
1886 / 1940?

Christianity may have originally come to Winchester during the Roman occupation, though evidence suggests that the town did not become a religious centre until Saxon times. Many of the kings of Wessex were buried in the Saxon Cathedral, the foundations of which can be seen on this side of the present building.

THE CATHEDRAL

The magnificent west front of Winchester Cathedral is seen here from its former burial ground. The beautifully-decorated Winchester Bible can be seen in the Cathedral Library. This 12th-century volume was hand-written by a single scribe over three years. The sumptuous decorations were prepared by several fine artists over a much longer period of time.

THE CATHEDRAL

1886 / 1940S

THE CATHEDRAL

1886 / 19403

Pilgrims came from all over the world to pay homage at the Shrine of St Swithun, a former Winchester Bishop. When the Saint's body was moved from the original burial place and into the Norman Cathedral, a violent storm broke out—perhaps the origin of St Swithun's influence over the British weather.

Buried in the Cathedral is Izaak Walton, author of 'The Compleat Angler', who died at his son-in-law's house in the Cathedral Close in 1683. A commemorative window was placed near to his tomb as a gift from the fishermen of England and America.

THE CATHEDRAL
WEST FRONT 1909 / 62178

Queen Mary I, 'Bloody Mary', married Philip of Spain in Winchester Cathedral during Stephen Gardiner's time as Bishop. This marriage was to lead to conflict between England and Spain during the subsequent reign of Mary's sister Elizabeth.

QUEEN MARY'S CHAIR

1911 / 63730

THE CATHEDRAL

1911 / 63722

A splendid view of Winchester Cathedral. The original Norman tower collapsed in 1107, some said because King William Rufus—a monarch not popular with the Church, though not really as bad as history has painted him—had been buried underneath it after being assassinated whilst hunting in the New Forest seven years earlier.

Jane Austen, the novelist, lies under a slab of marble in the north aisle of the Cathedral. She died at a house in College Street in 1817. Her tombstone shows no evidence of her being a writer—perhaps because it was considered to be an unsuitable employment for a woman at that time.

THE CATHEDRAL
1922 / 72488

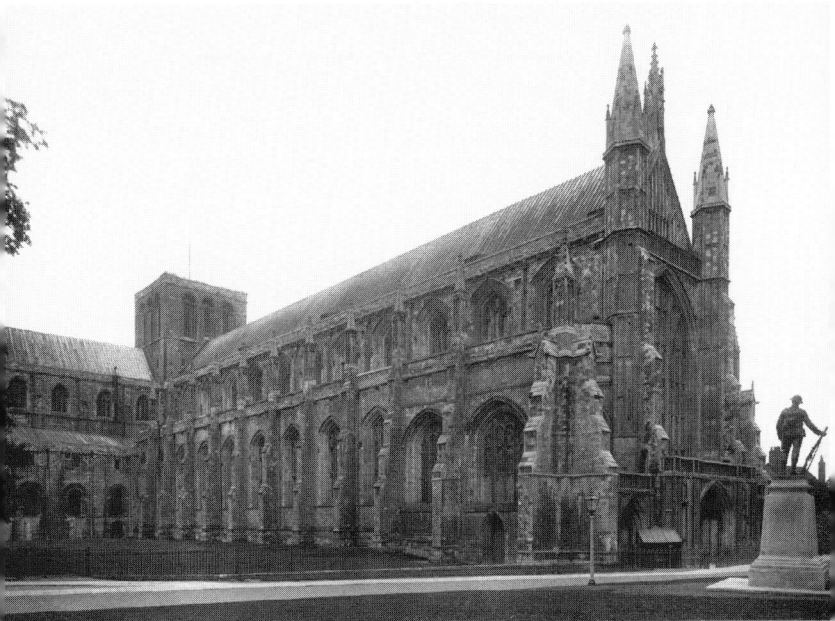

Winchester Cathedral was built on marshy ground, and by 1905 serious subsidence had occurred. A deep-sea diver, William Walker, was employed to go deep into the marshy water beneath and shore up the building. A bronze statuette commemorates the brave man who saved Winchester Cathedral.

THE CATHEDRAL

1922 / 72487

A stroll across the water meadows of the River Itchen brings the traveller to the village of St Cross, seen here just after the end of the First World War. One imagines that the small boy would have had some difficulty riding that particular bicycle.

ST CROSS VILLAGE

1919 / 68959

One visitor to St Cross was the poet John Keats, who stayed in Winchester during 1819 and often walked this way. It is said that his famous poem 'Ode to Autumn', which begins with the line 'Season of mists and mellow fruitfulness...', was written after one such ramble.

The Hospital of St Cross was founded by Bishop Henry de Blois, half-brother to King Stephen, in 1136. It is one of the oldest charitable establishments in England. Guided tours are available for those who visit this ancient site.

ST CROSS

1896 / 37250

The Church at St Cross was begun in the 1130s and serves as both the parish church and the Hospital's chapel. It too was founded by Henry de Blois, and is an excellent example of the development from Norman to Early English architecture.

ST CROSS CHURCH

1906 / 55879

ST CROSS HOSPITAL

1906 / 55884

This house of charity was founded to provide for the daily feeding of 100 poor men and the housing and clothing of 13 more who could no longer look after themselves. The Hospital is still home to some 25 Brothers, who now live in apartments within the original complex.

A second charitable foundation was made by Bishop Cardinal Beaufort in 1446: an Almshouse of Noble Poverty, for once-wealthy people who had fallen on hard times. Both foundations are represented at St Cross today, each with a different uniform— one red and one black.

ST CROSS

1909 / 61609

*A great deal of money was spent on the buildings of
this charitable foundation. The roof of the Great Hall
uses Spanish chestnut, while there is a great deal of
ornate wooden panelling and early stained glass.*

THE CHURCH OF ST CROSS

1919 / 68960

'Tickets for Sale' reads the sign to the left of the archway, as a member of the Brethren greets a visitor over eighty years ago. The tourist of today receives just as warm a welcome.

THE CHURCH OF ST CROSS

1919 / 68966

Every now and again, the Brothers gather in the mid 14th-century Brethren's Hall for a feast of celebration called the Gaudy Lunch.

ST CROSS HOSPITAL
THE BRETHREN 1928 / 80908

By the rules of the foundation, for eight centuries travellers have been given bread and ale on demand—the Wayfarers Dole. If you visit St Cross Hospital and ask—even today—you will be given a portion of bread and a beaker of ale. A delightful custom. May it long continue!

ST CROSS HOSPITAL
THE WAYFARERS DOLE 1928 / 80909

THE CHURCH OF ST CROSS

c1960 / W107177

A visit to St Cross breaks down the barrier between past and present; it is a chance to glimpse the charitable values of medieval England—and to pause for a while from the hurry and bustle of the 21st century.

CITY STREETS AND LANDMARKS

A good place to start an exploration of Winchester's streets is at the Buttercross, the 14th-century decorated monument that is everyone's favourite meeting place in the old city. How fortunate it was that the landowner who wished to remove the cross and use it as a garden ornament was thwarted by the loud protests of local people. Near here stood the Royal Palace of William the Conqueror. In the narrow passage leading from the Buttercross to the Square can be seen a column of stone; this is probably the last remaining portion of William's Winchester residence.

The Square itself is rich in history Originally part of what would have been the large cemetery of the nearby Cathedral, the Square became a venue for markets in the Middle Ages. It was also a place of execution, and the tolling of the bell of the Church of St Lawrence was the last sound to be heard by the unfortunates as their sentence was carried out. A plaque commemorates the execution of Lady Alice Lisle, who was brutally done to death here in 1685 for sheltering two rebels after the Duke of Monmouth's rebellion. Today the Square is a happier place of shops, restaurants and public houses, and benches to help take the weight off your feet as you tour Winchester.

The city mostly retains its medieval street pattern. A glance at the map produced by the cartographer John Speed in 1611 shows a town layout not very different to the one we know today. Certainly, by the end of the 12th century Winchester was second only to London in size, and it retained much of its old importance.

During the Anarchy, as the 'nineteen long winters' of King Stephen's reign is known, the city literally became a battleground between the King's half-brother Bishop Henry de Blois and Stephen's bitter enemy, the Empress Matilda. Winchester Castle was badly damaged and the old Norman Royal Palace was destroyed, and much of the town was burnt and razed to the ground during the siege and attack of 1141. Winchester took some years to recover.

Broadway and the High Street, which lead up from the River Itchen, may be sited along the route of an ancient trackway. The High Street of today ends at Westgate, one of two surviving medieval city gates in Winchester and a very prominent landmark. Its narrow archway had to cope with the demands of modern traffic until well into the 20th century. It is not only an excellent example of a fortification of its period, but contains also an informative museum and provides a viewpoint over much of the central part of the city.

There are several other lovely old buildings pictured in this section of the book. But they are just a sample of the joys of Winchester's building legacy, giving us a feeling that the Frith photographers were somewhat spoiled for choice. From the Tudor magnificence of God Begot House, to the gothic Victorian of the New Guildhall, Winchester is a dream come true for both the historian and the student of architecture.

But buildings and history alone do not make a city. In these photographs are the people of Winchester's more recent history - residents and tourists alike. Study the fashions of the day, and note the behaviour of the passers-by, from respectably-clad Victorians gossiping on a street corner to tiny boys posing for the camera, from the bicyclist to the driver of early motor cars, from policemen on watchful duty to window shoppers. These people are all a reminder that human nature, like the stones of old Winchester, never really changes.

CITY CROSS

1886 / 19443

The Buttercross is everyone's meeting place in Winchester; in the next few photographs we can see how the townscape around it changed over some seventy years. Notice in particular the transformation of the shops and businesses in the background.

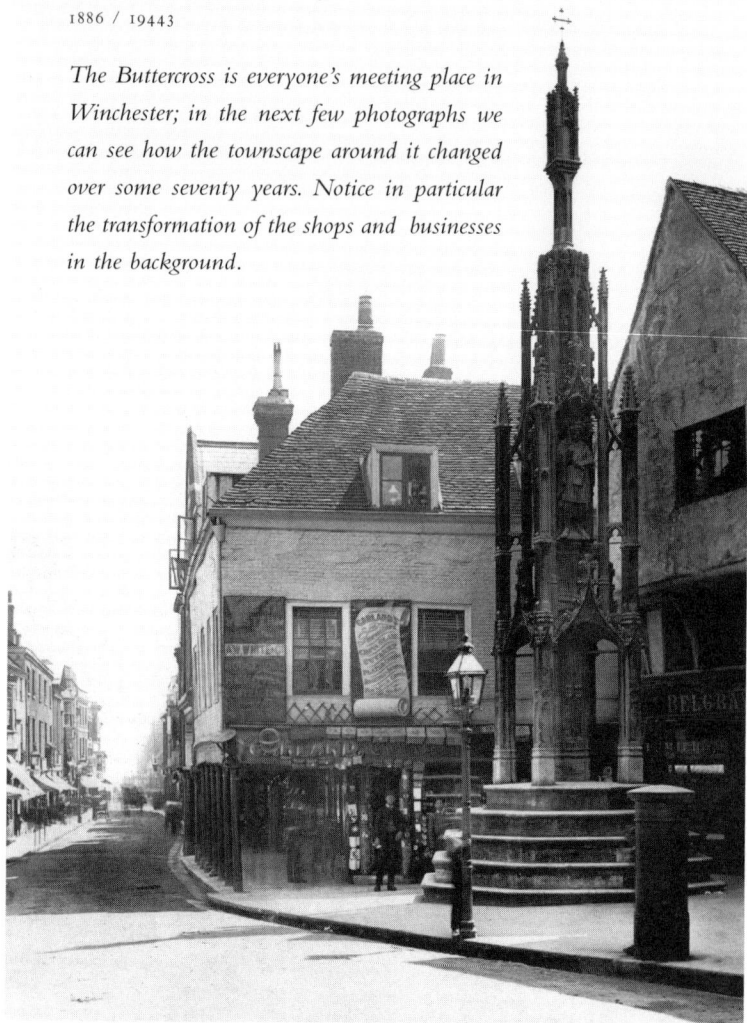

Buttercross dates from the 15th century. It almost disappeared in the 1700s, when it just escaped being sold to an influential local landowner as a garden ornament. Thanks to the angry protests of local people it remained in its original position.

CITY CROSS
1893 / 32655

By the end of the 19th century the building behind the cross had abandoned its role as a general store and had become a refreshment house. This must have been in recognition of Winchester's growing role as a tourist centre.

BUTTERCROSS

1899 / 43677

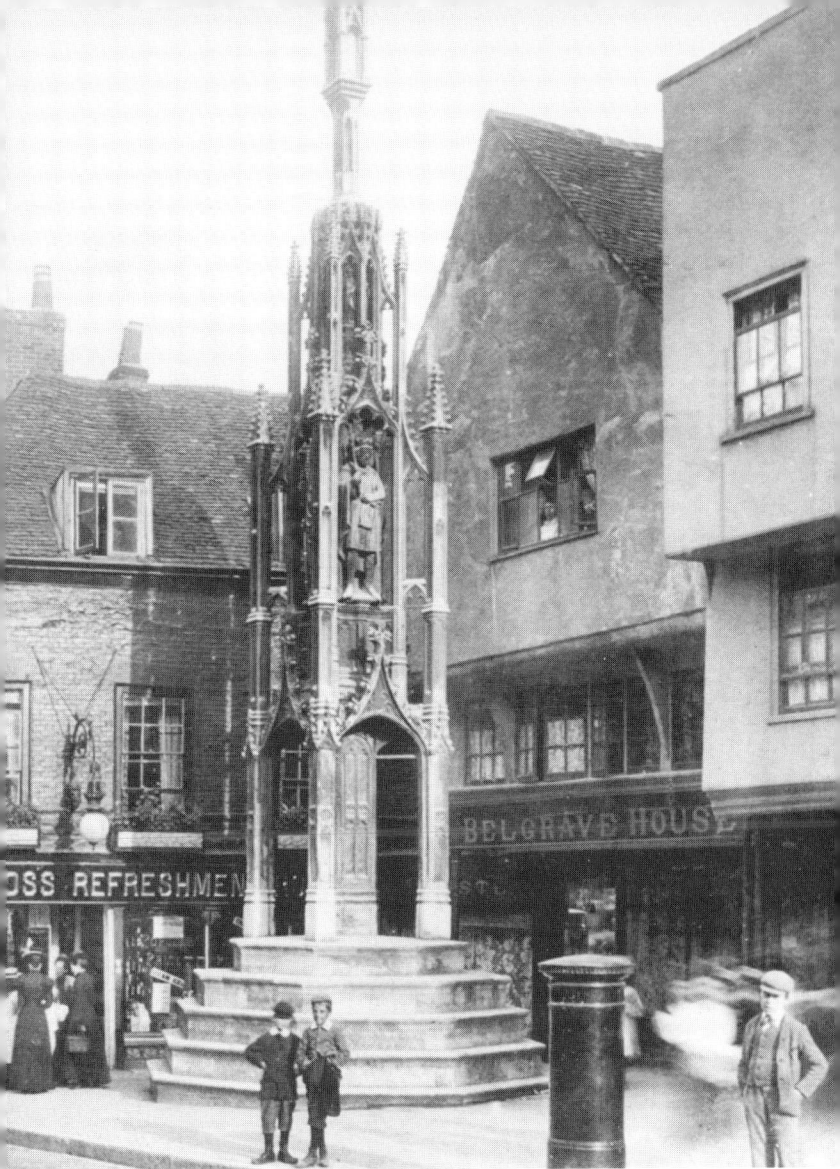

As the 'Tea' sign indicates, refreshments for passers-by were a part of Edwardian life in Winchester. But the main shop had become that most delightful of institutions—a traditional sweet shop.

HIGH STREET

1906 / 55856

44

Allen's Confectioners remained on the site when this photograph was taken in the 1950s. In the closing years of the 20th century, motor traffic became such a problem in the narrow roads of the old city that High Street was pedestrianised.

c1955 / W107066

High Street
1928 / 80882

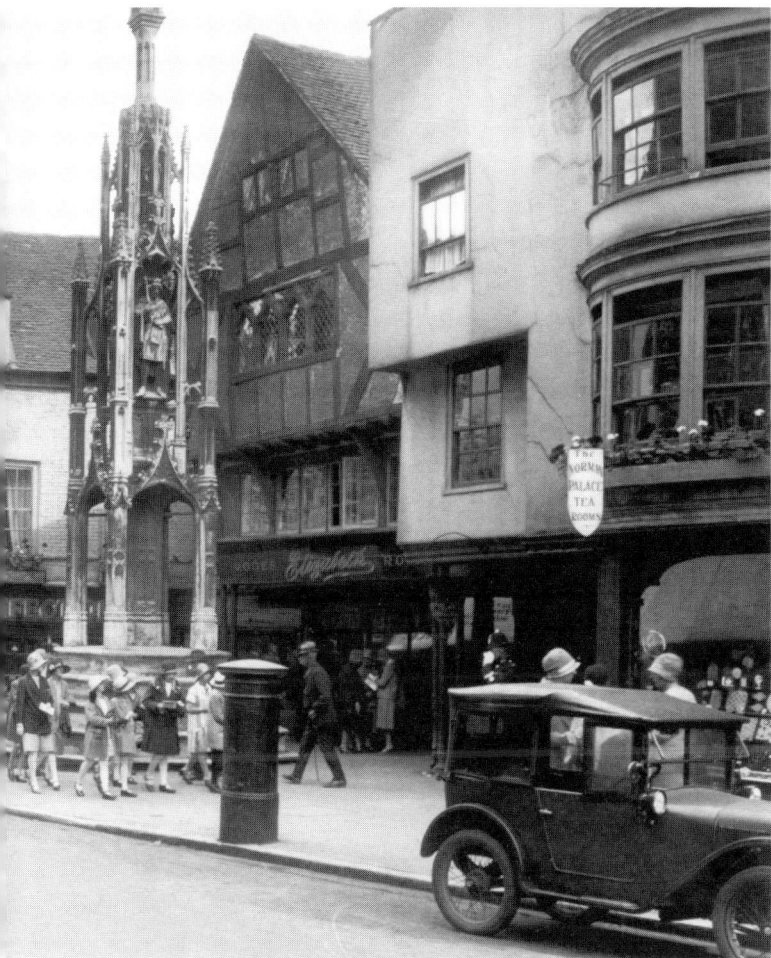

By the 1920s motor cars had largely replaced the horses and carts seen in the earlier photographs. It is interesting to note how, in the interests of fashion, everyone is wearing a hat. Can you spot the watchful city policeman?

The town clock, which has a statue of Queen Anne in a niche behind, was presented to the city after a royal visit in 1713. The building behind is the old Guildhall.

HIGH STREET
1899 / 43685

The covered walkway of The Pentice was created when the upper floor of its houses was extended in the 16th century. Until 1279 a Royal Mint of the Norman and Angevin kings stood on the site.

THE PENTICE

1928 / 80888

The Pentice
c1955 W107040

By the 1950s the habitual wearing of hats and caps might have become a fashion of the past, but strolling through the old streets of Winchester was increasing in popularity, as we can see from the large number of pedestrians.

HIGH STREET

1896 / 37243

A fine display of Victorian shop fronts can be seen in this photograph of the High Street, taken in the final years of the Queen's long reign. The line of this street dates back to the Roman town of Venta Belgarum, the market place of the Belgae, the Iron Age tribe who had been the original inhabitants.

Edwardians take a stroll along the upper end of High Street, with the old fortification of Westgate in view. Almost every monarch since William the Conqueror has passed this way

HIGH STREET

1906 / 55858

Westgate is one of the most prominent landmarks in Winchester. In the following pictures we see how it retains its importance as an historic and architectural feature as the city changes around it. Notice the old city wall pub, the Plume of Feathers, to the right of the gate.

WESTGATE
1896 / 37245

WESTGATE

Westgate dominated the western defences of the old city. It dates originally from the 12th century, and was reinforced during the Hundred Years War in anticipation of an attack by the French. The entire structure stands on the site of an earlier Roman fortification.

This view through Westgate's archway would have been glimpsed by generations of early travellers. Properly garrisoned medieval cities could sustain lengthy sieges by marauding armies.

WESTGATE AND HIGH STREET
1911 / 63747

Westgate has many of the hallmarks of a medieval defensive work, including 'murder holes' from which heavy weights or boiling oils and molten lead might be dropped during an attack, while the slits below the shields were used for firing early guns. A portcullis would have dropped down to close off the archway.

WESTGATE

1906 / 55860

For well over a century the room above Westgate's arch
has functioned as a small museum. It still houses the
excellent collection of historic weights and measures
and the instruments of torture shown here.

WESTGATE MUSEUM

1911 / 63748

FROM WESTGATE 1923 / 74230

Traffic climbs the hill from High Street towards Westgate. The kinds of traffic may change, but the importance of West;gate as a city monument remains. There must always have been excellent views towards Winchester Cathedral.

By the 1950s the Plume of Feathers was no more, and its site was derelict. As the warning notices indicate, 20th-century traffic was having difficulty coping with the narrow but historic arch.

WESTGATE

c1955 / W107057

This was the solution to the traffic problem. After several hundred years as the main western entrance to the town, Westgate was bypassed—the old Plume of Feathers became just a distant memory.

HIGH STREET

1909 / 62172

Not far from this part of the High Street is Staple Gardens, a street that predates even the Norman Conquest; it is Saxon in origin, dating to that glorious period when Winchester was the capital of Alfred's Kingdom of Wessex. An important wool market was held at Staple Gardens in the Middle Ages.

A walk down High Street from Westgate to the Buttercross takes the sightseer along one of the most ancient streets in the realm. On the right-hand side of the road, halfway down, is the old Guildhall, where the city's curfew bell is rung at 8pm each evening.

HIGH STREET

1909 / 62171

HIGH STREET
1928 / 80887

Here we see a policeman on point duty in the 1920s, coping with an increasing amount of traffic that began to bedevil Winchester's streets during the last century—a reminder that medieval streets were never designed with the motor car in mind.

HIGH STREET

1928 / 80886

A quarter of a century apart, this and the previous view of the High Street show how little it changed throughout the 20th century, with the exception of traffic problems and an increased number of tourists. Apart from the introduction of a pedestrianisation scheme and some new shop fronts, it remains much the same today.

The coming of the railway brought new prosperity to cities such as Winchester, encouraging tourism and new industries. The success of the Permanent Way led to a decline in the use of the old stagecoach routes—a decline not reversed until the heyday of the motor car.

Just across from Winchester Cathedral is The Square. In the background is the Norman church of St Lawrence, which tradition suggests was the chapel of William the Conqueror's royal palace. New Bishops of Winchester traditionally pray here before being enthroned.

THE SQUARE

1909 / 62174

Public executions were held in The Square in earlier days, with the bell of St Lawrence's tolling mournfully as the victim was brought before the crowd. The Square of today is a happier place, popular with those tourists who want a good view of the Cathedral.

THE SQUARE
1936 / 87173

St Giles Hill is the high ground to the east of the old city walls. A fine view over the city can be had by crossing the River Itchen and ascending to its summit. A famous fair used to be held on the hillside.

St Giles Hill
1899 / 42968

This late medieval building in Chesil Street is one of Winchester's oldest surviving buildings, dating from around 1450. It has served the city as a popular restaurant for many years.

THE OLDEST HOUSE (OLD CHESIL RECTORY)

1896 37247

The Old Chesil Rectory

c1955 / W107020

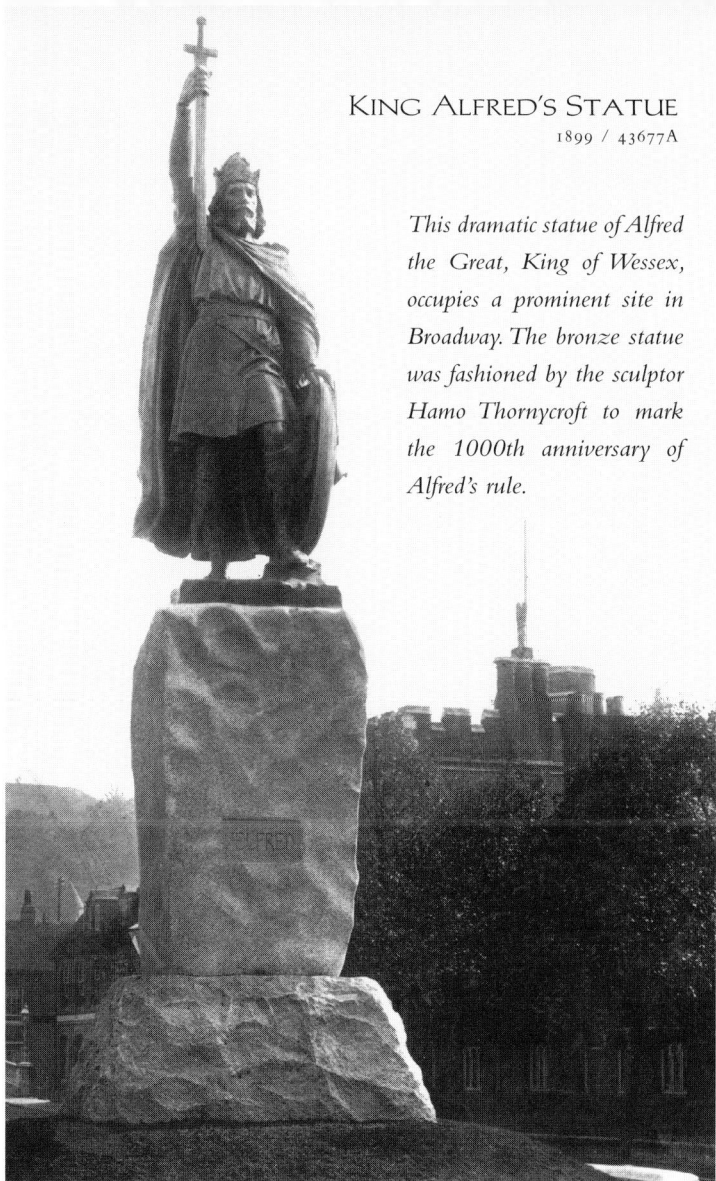

KING ALFRED'S STATUE

1899 / 43677A

This dramatic statue of Alfred the Great, King of Wessex, occupies a prominent site in Broadway. The bronze statue was fashioned by the sculptor Hamo Thornycroft to mark the 1000th anniversary of Alfred's rule.

Broadway and its continuation, the High Street, almost certainly follow the line of an ancient trackway that crossed the River Itchen during the Iron Age. It has remained the principal eastern approach to Winchester.

BROADWAY AND KING ALFRED'S STATUE

1909 / 61600

*Legend relates that the original city bridge
was built by St Swithun, the former Bishop
and patron saint of Winchester. The present
bridge dates back to 1813.*

CITY BRIDGE
1906 / 55867

WESTGATE AND NEW BUILDINGS
1896 / 37246

Victorian architects designed these buildings to be in considerable sympathy with the traditional buildings of Winchester. At the time that this photograph was taken, the corner building was the headquarters of the Hampshire Friendly Society.

THE ROUND TABLE
1906 / 55873

THE ROUND TABLE

1906 / 55873

The Round Table of King Arthur, made supposedly by the magician Merlin, has hung in Winchester's Great Hall for some six hundred years. In fact, it was probably made in the 13th century and restored in Tudor times, when the face of a young Henry VIII was added to the portrait of the legendary Arthur.

The present Great Hall of Winchester Castle was rebuilt during the reign of Henry III. When the castle was demolished, the hall was kept as a courtroom; it was here that Sir Walter Raleigh was sentenced to death in 1603.

THE GREAT HALL

1912 / 64458

GOD BEGOT HOUSE

1909 / 62177

Kingsgate, surmounted by the little church of St Swithun-upon-Kingsgate, is one of just two surviving medieval gateways at Winchester. Just around the corner from here is the house where the novelist Jane Austen died.

KINGSGATE

The present God Begot House is Tudor, though it stands on the site of an ancient manor originally bequeathed by Emma, widow of King Canute, to the Priory of St Swithun in 1052. Lawbreakers could seek sanctuary at God Begot House during the Middle Ages.

YE OLDE HOSTEL OF GOD BEGOT

1929 / 81625

THE HOSPITAL

1906 / 55876

As an important cathedral city, Winchester established an important tradition of tending the sick, probably from the days when pilgrims came to the shrine of St Swithun in search of miraculous cures. We see here fine examples of Victorian architecture.

ABBEY GARDENS
1923 / 74232

R.H.C. HOSPITAL

1909 / 61604

The gardens of many of these erstwhile charitable foundations are havens of peace and tranquillity, away from the bustle of the city. Some visitors still emulate the old tradition of making a personal pilgrimage to the city of Winchester.

ST JOHN'S ALMSHOUSE
1911 / 63740

CHRIST'S HOSPITAL

1911 / 63742

Near to the site of the Guildhall once stood the Nunnaminster, one of the three royal monasteries of Saxon Winchester, founded in about 903 by Ealhswith, the widow of Alfred the Great.

THE GUILDHALL
1936 / 87172

A monument to Victorian self-confidence, the Guildhall is built in the popular Gothic revival style and was opened in 1873. Today it is a favourite venue for artistic events and conferences.

THE GUILDHALL
1886 / 19423

ROUND AND ABOUT

Travellers of all kinds have passed through the countryside around Winchester for a variety of reasons, from Iron Age warriors to Roman legionnaires, medieval pilgrims, sailors and merchants to the tourists of today. Many still find their way to the ancient capital of Wessex, and for just as many reasons: some deliberately to view the beautiful Cathedral and other historic buildings in the city, others to buy goods from an impressive array of modern shops, or maybe just to explore the countryside and the towns and villages thereabouts.

Winchester College is the oldest public school in England, founded by William of Wykeham in 1382, with a dedication to the Virgin Mary. 'Manners Makyth Man' runs the school motto, and time spent in Winchester probably does much good in shaping the characters of the pupils—or Wykehamists, as they are called. Perhaps it gives them all an abiding interest in the history and architecture of the Middle Ages, if nothing else. Scholars in olden times led a Spartan existence; electricity was only introduced in 1930, and for another thirty years the boys had to bathe in tin baths filled with cold water.

Guided walks take the interested visitor around several of the college buildings, which have been used since its foundation and are still in use today. There might be a chance, if the timing is right, to hear the singing of the college choir, supplemented by the younger quiristers from the

Pilgrims School—the Cathedral's choir school—echoing out of the 14th-century college chapel.

A ramble across the water meadows of the Itchen to the downlands above will show the walker just how old this landscape is. On St Catherine's Hill is a famous Iron Age hillfort, while further out are Bronze Age barrows, Roman roads and villa sites.

Thanks to their proximity to Winchester and the larger city of Southampton, many of the towns and villages grew considerably in size during the 20th century, but all are worthy of exploration. A pretty walk—if the modern roads can be avoided—is the journey to the Worthies. Both Headbourne Worthy and Kings Worthy have been developed since these photographs were taken, but they are well worth a visit. Headbourne Worthy has an excellent Saxon church, much of it older than the neighbouring Winchester Cathedral. Tradition alleges that the Saxon Wilfrid built the first place of worship here on this site, though some of the building might date from the reign of Edward the Confessor. After the Reformation Henry VIII gave the Worthies to his one beloved queen, Jane Seymour.

A longer walk to the south of Winchester brings the visitor to Twyford, situated like its larger neighbour on a particularly old crossing point over the River Itchen. The 'Queen of Hampshire Villages' was also increased in size and population since these photographs were taken, but as an historic a Saxon settlement, and given its connections with the poet and satirist Alexander Pope, should be visited.

The River Itchen has helped shape the destinies of many of the communities along its banks; it should be followed from source to mouth, halting at each settlement along the journey—this would be a most interesting way to get a grasp of the social history of this part of England. From its prettiest water meadows and the heights of the downs come distant views of Winchester and its Cathedral—seen in the way that pilgrims of the past would have first regarded the 'city of kings and priests'.

Here we see an empty street on the approaches to Winchester during the long 'afternoon' of Edward VII's reign. Notice the absence of any traffic, apart from one solitary horse and cart—the streets around the city are a little more crowded a century later.

STREET SCENE

1906 / 53493

WINCHESTER COLLEGE
RIDDING FIELD 1919 / 68956

These are the playing fields of Winchester College. Winchester College was founded by William of Wykeham in 1387, and is the oldest public school in England. The college was originally founded to prepare 70 poor scholars for entry to New College, Oxford, and then for the priesthood.

Until the 1960s, Winchester's pupils led a Spartan existence, bathing every day in cold water in tin baths; perhaps this helped generations of schoolboys to face the rigours of life outside and to live up to the school motto: 'Manners Makyth Man'.

WINCHESTER COLLEGE FROM THE CATHEDRAL

1929 / 81611

Many of the original buildings of Winchester College remain, and are still used by today's pupils. The college chapel was originally consecrated around the year 1394. In the cloister nearby is the grave of Field Marshall Lord Wavell—one of a distinguished line of 'old boys'.

WINCHESTER COLLEGE
1922 / 72493

Romsey Road leads westward away from the city centre and towards the rolling downlands of Hampshire. Winchester is an excellent touring centre for exploring one of the most ancient landscapes in Britain.

STANMORE FROM ROMSEY ROAD

1928 / 80896

In Hursley church, southwest of Winchester, lies the body of Richard Cromwell, the famous 'Tumbledown Dick' of history, who succeeded his father Oliver Cromwell as Lord Protector of England for a few months before the restoration of King Charles II.

HURSLEY
THE CHURCH 1886 / 19446

Winchester has always been an important centre for military training; much of the countryside round and about is used for tactical exercises. The barracks, close to Westgate, contain several interesting military museums.

THE BARRACKS
c1960 / W107111

The church of Headbourne Worthy is one of the oldest in southern England: it stood for long years before William the Conqueror won the realm at the Battle of Hastings in 1066. In the churchyard lies the Stuart scholar Joseph Bingham, author of a famous work on Christian antiquities.

HEADBOURNE WORTHY
THE CHURCH AND THE LYCHGATE 1912 / 64462

On the old highway leading north out of Winchester is Kings Worthy, a large village of considerable antiquity. The church has been sympathetically restored, though the flint tower is 15th-century.

KINGS WORTHY
THE CHURCH 1912 / 64469

In the churchyard is the grave of the great Victorian Liberal Shaw Lefevre, Lord Eversley, who worked closely with the long-serving Prime Minister Mr Gladstone. Lefevre was a people's champion, for he defended public footpaths and common lands. He was born in the reign of William IV and died aged 97 during the reign of George V.

KINGS WORTHY
THE CHURCH AND THE LYCHGATE 1912 / 64468

In this village in the early years of the last century lived four brothers, Ernest, Cecil, Reginald and Charles Baring. All four lost their lives in the First World War. A plaque in the church marks their tragic passing.

KINGS WORTHY
THE VILLAGE 1912 / 64467

Above the banks of the River Itchen stands Avington Mansion. Many of the grand country houses, parks and estates of Hampshire are now popular attractions, within easy travelling distance of Winchester.

KINGS WORTHY
AVINGTON MANSION c1960 / K143009

An ancient yew tree shows the antiquity of many a country churchyard. Yew was used in the manufacture of the traditional English longbow, which turned the tide of battle at Crecy and Agincourt.

TWYFORD

THE 1000-YEAR-OLD YEW TREE c1955 / T284004

The 'Queen of Hampshire Villages', Twyford, now a very large settlement, belonged to the See of Winchester from Saxon times. The poet Alexander Pope attended school here, and was expelled for lampooning his schoolmaster in verse.

TWYFORD
HIGH STREET c1955 / T284010

One 18th-century resident of Twyford was Mrs Maria Fitzherbert, who spent much of her childhood here, before going to London and becoming the mistress of the Prince of Wales—later George IV. Local tradition alleges that she married Prince George in secret at nearby Brambridge House.

TWYFORD
QUEEN STREET c1965 / T284014

The local school is at the heart of many an English community, being used for many local occasions after the end of the school day.

TWYFORD
THE CHURCH OF ENGLAND SCHOOL c1965 / T284024

TWYFORD
QUEEN STREET AND THE VOLUNTEER INN c1965 / T284026

Twyford, as the name suggests, stands on an ancient crossing place over the River Itchen. The downlands hereabouts bear the marks of Iron Age dwellers who occupied this valley three thousand years ago.

TWYFORD
THE CHURCH FROM THE RIVER ITCHEN
c1965 / T284032

The 140-ft tower and spire of Twyford Church dominate the banks of the nearby River Itchen. This is a pleasant place to sit on a summer's evening, and admire the ancient landscape that makes Winchester and Hampshire such a delightful place to visit.

INDEX

PLEASE HELP US BRING FRITH'S PHOTOGRAPHS TO LIFE

Our authors do their best to recount the history of the places they write about. They give insights into how particular towns and villages developed, they describe the architecture of streets and buildings, and they discuss the lives of famous people who lived there. But however knowledgeable our authors are, the story they tell is necessarily incomplete.

Frith's photographs are so much more than plain historical documents. They are living proofs of the flow of human life down the generations. They show real people at real moments in history; and each of those people is the son or daughter of someone, the brother or sister, aunt or uncle, grandfather or grandmother of someone else. All of them lived, worked and played in the streets depicted in Frith's photographs.

We would be grateful if you would tell us about the many places shown in our photographs—the streets with their buildings, shops, businesses and industries. Describe your own memories of life in those streets: what it was like growing up there, who ran the local shop and what shopping was like years ago; if your workplace is shown tell us about your working day and what the building is used for now. With your help more and more Frith photographs can be brought to life, and vital memories preserved for posterity.

We will gradually add your comments and stories to the archive for the benefit of historians of the future. Wherever possible, we will try to include some of your comments in future editions of our books. Moreover, if you spot errors in dates, titles or other facts, please let us know, because our archive records are not always completely accurate—they rely on 150 years of human endeavour and hand-compiled records.

So please write, fax or email us with your stories and memories. Thank you!

FREE PRINT OF YOUR CHOICE

Choose any Frith photograph in this book.
Simply complete the Voucher opposite and return it with your remittance for £2.25 (to cover postage and handling) and we will print the photograph of your choice in SEPIA (size 11 x 8 inches) and supply it in a cream mount with a burgundy rule line (overall size 14 x 11inches).

Please note: photographs with a reference number starting with a "Z" are not Frith photographs and cannot be supplied under this offer.

Offer valid for delivery to UK addresses only.

Mounted Print
Overall size 14 x 11 inches (355 x 280mm)

PLUS: **Order additional Mounted Prints at HALF PRICE - £7.49 each** (normally £14.99)
If you would like to order more Frith prints from this book, possibly as gifts for friends and family, you can buy them at half price (with no additional postage and handling costs).

PLUS: **Have your Mounted Prints framed**
For an extra £14.95 per print you can have your mounted print(s) framed in an elegant polished wood and gilt moulding, overall size 16 x 13inches (no additional postage and handling required).

IMPORTANT!

These special prices are only available if you use this form to order. You must use the ORIGINAL VOUCHER on this page (no copies permitted).

We can only despatch to one address. This offer cannot be combined with any other offer.

FRITH PRODUCTS AND SERVICES

All Frith photographs are available for you to buy as framed or mounted prints. From time to time, other illustrated items such as Address Books, Calendars, Table Mats are also available. Already, almost 50,000 Frith archive photographs can be viewed and purchased on the internet through the Frith website.

For more detailed information on Frith companies and products, visit:

www.francisfrith.co.uk

For further information, trade, or author enquiries, contact:

The Francis Frith Collection, Frith's Barn, Teffont, Salisbury SP3 5QP

Tel: +44 (0) 1722 716 376 Fax: +44 (0) 1722 716 881 Email: sales@francisfrith.co.uk

Voucher

for FREE and Reduced Price Frith Prints

Do not photocopy this voucher. Only the original is valid, so please fill it in, cut it out and return it to us with your order.

	Picture ref no	Page number	Qty	Mounted @ £7.49 UK	Framed + £14.95	UK orders Total £
1			1	Free of charge*	£	£
2				£7.49	£	£
3				£7.49	£	£
4				£7.49	£	£
5				£7.49	£	£
6				£7.49	£	£
Please allow 28 days for delivery				* Post & handling (UK)		£2.25
				Total Order Cost		£

Title of this book . . . .

I enclose a cheque / postal order for £ . . . .
payable to 'The Francis Frith Collection'

OR debit my Mastercard / Visa / Switch (Maestro) / Amex card

(credit cards please on all overseas orders), details below

Card Number

Issue No (Switch only)   Valid from (Amex/Switch)

Expires   Signature

Name Mr/Mrs/Ms . . . .
Address . . . .
. . . .
. . . .
. . . . .Postcode. . . . .
Daytime Tel No . . . .
E-mail . . . .

Valid to 31/12/07